Apes & Monkeys

Published in 2007 in the U.S.A by Dalmatian Press, LLC
Text Copyright © 2007 Dalmatian Press, LLC
Art Copyright © 2007 Edizioni Larus S.p.A.
All rights reserved

The DALMATIAN PRESS name and logo are trademarks of
Dalmatian Press, LLC, Atlanta Georgia 30329. No part of this book may be reproduced
or copied in any form without the written permission of Dalmatian Press.

Printed in U.S.A. • ISBN: 1-40373-236-1

07 08 09 10 9 8 7 6 5 4 3 2 1

Gorilla

Gorillas, the biggest apes in the world, can weigh as much as 450 pounds! They have black fur and large heads to support strong neck and jaw muscles.

Gorillas live in small groups, led by grown-up males striped with silver fur. Leaders look for food, walking miles a day on all fours, leaning on their knuckles. And they protect their families by pretending to attack—standing, ripping up bushes, and pounding on their chests while yelling!

Big gorillas sleep on the ground at night. Youngsters and females snooze in the trees.

Did You Know?
A gorilla's arms are always longer than its legs!

Baby Gorillas

Gorillas have babies about every three years. Babies are cuddled and carried by all the females, but they sleep next to their mothers. When the mother wakes up, the baby jumps on her back and rides along! Then, when the group stops, all babies wrestle together, slide down damp, grassy banks, or climb trees.

In a few months, they're scampering on all fours, and at seven months they're climbing trees!

Baby gorillas are all grown up when they turn three.

CREATURE FEATURE:
Newborn gorillas can't hold onto their mothers, so each mother hugs her baby tight.

What does it eat?
Gorillas are herbivores. That means they eat mostly plants—soft shoots, young twigs, and juicy leaves.

Chimpanzee

Chimpanzees are very smart—clever enough to make tools!

Chimps live in the forest in tribes as big as forty. A male—not the strongest, but the most expert—leads each group.

Chimpanzees are great at climbing, but mostly hang out on the ground looking for things to eat. When it gets dark, they shimmy up trees and make safe little dens by bending branches and tearing off leaves.

What does it eat?
Fruit and seeds, and bananas! They can gobble up to 50 bananas just for lunch! Also leaves, plant rinds, sprouts, insects, and small mammals.

Baby Chimpanzees

A mother chimp gives birth to her baby in a secret place, alone. After the baby is born, the baby wants milk and sucks its thumb, just like a little girl or boy!

Mothers keep their babies close for three years. When the mother moves, her baby hangs on to her furry lap. Later, little chimps ride "piggyback." Then, when they're big enough, they walk beside their mothers.

For three years, a mother shows her baby how to eat, be part of a tribe, and protect itself from danger. Then the little one leaves to spend more time with chimps its own age.

CREATURE FEATURE: With all its face muscles, a chimpanzee can show emotions like sadness and joy.

Did You Know? Chimpanzees like to eat termites!

Guenon

Guenons are monkeys that live in groups of about forty. They like to hang out in trees where it's safe. And when these monkeys are thirsty, they just lick rainwater from leaves!

> **CREATURE FEATURE:**
> Guenons have tough skin on their bottoms so they can sit on branches for a long time!

Baby Guenons

A little guenon holds on tight to its mother's fur to keep from falling; and the mother clings to her baby as she swings through the trees. Baby guenons stay close to their mothers, who protect and care for them and teach them everything they will need to know as grown-ups.

What does it eat?
Guenons are omnivores—they eat more than plants. They fill up on leaves, shoots, and fruits, but they also eat insects.

Putty-Nose Guenon

The putty-nose guenon likes forests that aren't thick. He is very gentle.

Vervet Guenon

The vervet lives near the *savanna* (a grassy plain), and eats insects, lizards, and fruits. He screams special alarms, too! Then, other monkeys nearby will know if the enemy is a leopard, an eagle, or a snake.

Dwarf Guenon

The dwarf, the smallest African monkey, lives in swampy forests. He soaks manioc plants in water and eats them when all the poison is washed out.

De Brazza Guenon

This monkey has a hairy white chin and a red mark on his forehead. He lives along riverbanks and eats tropical lizards called geckoes.

Mustached Guenon

This little monkey likes thick forests. He hangs out in trees up to 80 feet high, and only eats fruit.

Did You Know?

A guenon's tail tells you how it feels: A straight tail means the monkey is afraid. A tail hooked up toward the chest says a guenon feels safe.

Mandrill

Mandrills have long faces and bright blue and red fur. They live on the edge of forests and spend most of their time looking for food, as well as "talking" to each other with grunts and cries.

Mandrills live in tribes with a male leader that is old but strong. He defends them from enemies like leopards, large snakes, and eagles.

Did You Know?

At night, mandrills climb into trees and sleep safely in the branches.

Baby Mandrills

When a baby mandrill is born, the mother nurses it and looks after it carefully. She also lets other females "baby-sit" the little mandrill to teach them how to look after their own little ones someday.

Mandrills groom each other, not only to keep clean but also to stay close.

CREATURE FEATURE: The Mandrill is a monkey, but its name means "man-ape."

When a male mandrill sees an enemy, his face, chest, and hands become even brighter. He flings out his arms, tips back his head, and opens his mouth to show long, sharp teeth. Even leopards get scared!

What does it eat?
Roots and tubers, fruits, shoots, and plants, as well as insects, worms, snails, frogs, and lizards.

Colobus Monkey

Baby Colobuses

A newborn colobus is all white. Its mother hugs it close with one arm as she swings through the trees. After a week, the baby holds on to its mother's back.

CREATURE FEATURE:
The colobus does not have a real thumb—only a stump with no nail.

What does it eat?
Fruits, leaves, seeds and tender shoots, as well as small animals and insects. He loves juniper berries!

The colobus is one of the most beautiful monkeys in Africa. It is a soft, velvety black with a cloak of long, white fur. The colobus lives in the highest African tree-tops. It is shy and gentle, and runs away at the first hint of danger, scurrying fast from branch to branch.

Did You Know?
The colobus has a black face with white fur trim that looks like a long beard. This helps him move unseen in darkness, as well as bright light.

Baboon

The baboon is a big monkey that lives in the African savanna. It has a long face and strong teeth that it bares at enemies such as leopards. A baboon walks on all fours on its palms and soles. Every day these monkeys walk three miles looking for food, but they still take time to groom each other, making friendships stronger.

What does it eat?
Grasses, fruits, and tubers, as well as insects and birds—and sometimes hares and small gazelles.

Baby Baboons

A newborn clings tightly to its mother's chest. Later, the youngster balances on his mother's back. Mother baboons are loving, but the whole tribe looks after little ones.

Did You Know?
A baboon tribe can have as many as 200 members!

Orangutan

The orangutan is the largest tree-dwelling animal. Its Malaysian name means "man of the forest" because this ape looks a little like a human. In fact, an adult male can be as big as a man. An orangutan's face shows feelings, such as fear, happiness, and sadness.

Orangutans don't live in tribes. They like to live alone in the forests of Sumatra and Borneo. The orangutan spends most of the day looking for food.

The orangutan is also one of the largest mammals in danger of *extinction* (dying out). People are now teaching baby orangutan orphans how to survive in the forest.

What does it eat?
Mainly fruits, but leaves, shoots, small animals, and eggs, too.

Baby Orangutans

Mothers have only one baby at a time. They look after each baby orangutan for six or seven years. The first year, the baby stays with its mother, nursing on milk and hanging on to her long fur. Then it begins to play and move around in the trees. Step by step, the little orangutan recognizes food and learns how to survive.

CREATURE FEATURE:
An orangutan's long, reddish fur makes it easy to spot.

Did You Know?
Orangutans are very clever. They find solutions to problems, like using big leaves as umbrellas when it rains.

Gibbon

Gibbons are lively apes always on the move. They have round heads and flat faces that look almost human. And they walk upright on two legs!

Gibbons, however, also have very long arms that they use to swing perfectly through the trees. In fact, a gibbon's arms are so long that they touch the ground when the gibbon is standing up straight!

Gibbons like to get into groups and yell loudly. They scream mostly at dawn and when the sun sets. Each group has its own calls.

What does it eat?
Fruit, tender twigs and shoots, small birds, insects, and spiders.

CREATURE FEATURE:
Like all other apes, gibbons do not have tails!

Siamang

The siamang is an unusual gibbon, about three feet tall with black fur. It has a sack of stretchy skin on its throat, which helps it make loud cries that can be heard miles away.

Since it's so big and heavy, this gibbon moves through the trees more carefully than its "cousins" and hangs on to two limbs at all times.

Siamang
Hoolock

Hoolock

The hoolock is one of the smallest gibbons. It's easy to spot because of its dark fur with the white stripe on its forehead.

This ape does not like cool weather or very high places. He's livelier than the siamang and covers more ground looking for food.

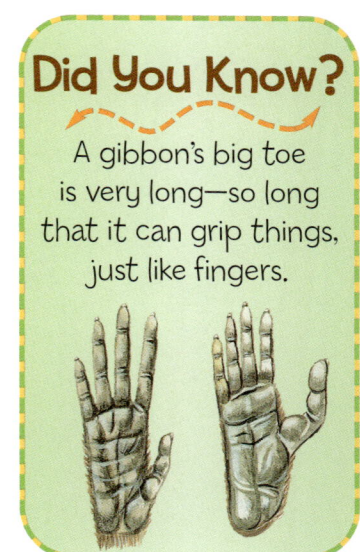

Did You Know?

A gibbon's big toe is very long—so long that it can grip things, just like fingers.

Proboscis Monkey

The proboscis monkey gets its name from the male's big nose! (Proboscis means snout or nose.) When the monkey screams, his nose probably makes the shouting louder.

Females are smaller than males, but both have tails as long as their bodies. Proboscis monkeys have chestnut or reddish fur on their backs, with lighter bellies and shoulders.

This friendly monkey lives along the coast or in riverbank forests, where it spends most of its time in trees, hanging out in groups of about thirty.

The proboscis is a daylight animal and is busies in the morning, when it makes a call that sounds like "kahau."

Proboscis monkeys like the young leaves and shoots of trees called mangroves and pedadas. These only grow on riverbanks and along the coast of the island of Borneo. A small part of their diet also comes from fruits and flowers.

Since leaves are not very nutritious, the monkey has to eat a lot! But these leaves take a long time to digest, so the proboscis monkey often has a round, swollen belly.

CREATURE FEATURE:
Very long tails help proboscis monkeys balance their bodies when they jump.

Proboscis monkeys are lazy, spending hours barely moving while chewing their food. But they can shoot through the trees when they sense danger!

Since proboscis monkeys live in coastal or river-bank forests, they are also great swimmers. Some have even been seen swimming in the sea, far, far away from the coast.

Did You Know?

Strange tales are told about the proboscis monkey. One legend says that the monkey covers its nose when it jumps from tree to tree so it won't bump its nose on the branches!

Hanuman Langur

The Hanuman langur is thin, with long limbs and a three-foot tail. He lives in the trees, where it's easier to hide from danger, and is so good at climbing that he loves buildings—particularly Hindu temples!

The most common monkey in India, the Hanuman lives closely with humans. Indians even train them for street shows!

A troop of langurs has dozens of members and is run by a dominant male.

CREATURE FEATURE:
The Hanuman langur can jump fifteen feet high!

Baby Langurs

When a baby langur is born, it climbs onto its mother's belly and is cradled in her arms. The baby lives mostly on mother's milk, but after three months, it begins to try eating leaves.

Did You Know?

To Hindus, this monkey is the symbol of a "god-monkey" called Hanuman.

Langur monkeys have many "cousins." Each one is special, since different kinds of fur create beards, whiskers, and hairstyles around the monkeys' faces.

Spectacled Langur

This monkey has pale skin around its eyes. Monkeys use facial muscles to signal each other, and the spectacled langur's "mask" is lively!

White-bearded Langur

This monkey has thick, white fur on its cheeks. It is nimble and can run as fast as 20 mph (miles per hour)!

Douc Langur

This langur has fur in colored patches, so it looks like it's dressed in a jacket, pants, shoes, socks, and a vest!

CREATURE FEATURE: Langur monkeys just love to rest in the sun, but can move very fast—in trees or on the ground—at the first hint of danger!

Did You Know?
Monkeys and apes are not color-blind. Some have patches of skin in colors, like red and blue.

Golden Snub-nosed Monkey

Golden Snub-nosed Monkey
Himalayan Langur

This rare monkey has a lovely thick, soft coat of golden-red. He lives in trees and can be found in bamboo forests, as far up as snowfields.

Troops of as many as a hundred of these monkeys often come down from the trees to rummage for shoots, bamboo, leaves, and fruits.

Himalayan Langur

This monkey can be found in very high woods. It stays near rocky areas, particularly if running water is nearby, and lives in groups of about forty. It is very nimble, and can jump as far as thirty-five feet!

The young spend their first four years playing, and then learn the rules of the tribe—including how to keep out of trouble.

Did You Know?

Local folks in China call this animal the "snow monkey."

Howler Monkey

The biggest monkey of the Americas is called a "howler" because of its loud screams. These monkeys sometimes can be heard as far as three miles away! The powerful yells are a way of marking the monkey's territory.

The howler, which weighs up to 20 pounds, likes to stay in trees, moving its long, thick limbs carefully from one branch to the next.

Uakari

This small to medium-sized monkey has a long, orange-colored coat, a bald, rounded head, and cheeks that are red. And when the uakari is upset, its face gets even redder! It lives mainly in the flooded areas of the Amazon, in large tribes.

It is not unusual to see this monkey hanging upside down by its feet, using its hands to collect food.

Spider Monkey

The spider monkey got its name from its delicate body and long, thin limbs. It has a prickly, rough pelt and a long tail that works like a hook, helping the monkey leap from branch to branch.

It's a great gymnast in the branches, and can jump as far as 40 feet!

CREATURE FEATURE:
A long tail not only keeps the spider monkey balanced, but is useful for picking fruit, too!

Baby Spider Monkeys

Most spider monkey babies are born in the fall. When the baby is young and the mother begins to move, the little spider monkey clasps the mother's fur and winds its tail around the base of its mother's tail.

What does it eat?
Palm nuts and fruits from tropical trees. They also poke around in tree trunks for insects, and love tender shoots, flowers, and leaves.

Did You Know?
The spider monkey's body is made to swing around treetops. Its thumbs are stumps, and its fingers are long and bent, so the monkey can grip branches safely and quickly.

Tamarin

The tamarin is one of the smallest American monkeys—only one pound and about ten inches tall. But its tail is longer than its body!

The tamarin has a mane of backswept white hairs surrounding its face, and when it fights, the male's mane stands up to make it look stronger and taller.

Baby Tamarins

Unlike most monkeys, the mother tamarin often gives birth to twins. Little ones hang on to their mothers when nursing, but when the family moves, the male carries the babies on his back.

Squirrel Monkey

This little monkey weighs only about 35 ounces. A loveable animal with a round head and big eyes, the squirrel monkey lives in large tribes up in the treetops. When jumping from branch to branch, the monkey uses its long tail for balance.

CREATURE FEATURE:
The squirrel monkey likes to crack walnuts and eggs by smashing them against branches.

What does it eat?
The squirrel monkey really likes fruit, but also eats leaves and shoots, eggs, lizards, and insects found in tree trunks.

Owl Monkey

The small owl monkey is covered with a thick gray-and-brown coat, so it can blend in with trees. It also has long, strong fingers with thumbs.

Owl monkeys live in couples or small family groups. During the day, the family sleeps side-by-side in hollow trees.

Did You Know?
This is the only monkey that is nocturnal (meaning it stays awake at night). It has very big eyes.

Woolly Monkey

This monkey sleeps sitting on a branch! He wraps a long tail around his body and the branch, so he won't fall off.

What does it eat?
Mainly fruits, which it picks by using its tail like a hand.

Good night, monkeys!